This Book Is a Comp[lete] Study Guide to the Online Course.

How to Perform Deck Inspections

InterNACHI Members: Take the free, online *How to Perform Deck Inspections* course now (free to InterNACHI members)

The course is free to all InterNACHI® members.

Upon successfully completing the online course and passing the final exam, you will receive a Certificate of Completion and be able to:

- list and describe the major components of a deck;

- distinguish between proper and improper installation techniques;

- identify and describe common major structural and safety problems; and

- communicate to a client indications of defects.

Take the online course at **www.nachi.org/deck-inspections-course**

How to Perform Deck Inspections

This publication is intended to teach the student how to inspect residential wood decks and balconies. It does not address the inspection of decks and balconies that are constructed with plastic, composites, or any other material other than solid-sawn lumber.

This guide focuses on single-level residential and commercial wood decks. The recommendations found within this publication exceed the requirements of both InterNACHI's Home Inspection Standards of Practice and the International Standards of Practice for Inspecting Commercial Properties.

This guide may also serve as a reference manual for onsite inspections of wood decks, as well as a study aid for InterNACH's online Deck Inspections course and final exam.

To order additional training books, visit www.InspectorOutlet.com

Author:

Nick Gromicko, Founder, International Association of Certified Home Inspectors

Graphics:

Lisaira Vega, Levi Nelson, Jackson Tupper & Erica Saurey

Editor:

Kate Tarasenko / Crimea River

Layout & Design:

Jessica Langer

www.NACHI.org

Table of Contents

Introduction

More than 2 million decks are built and replaced each year in North America. InterNACHI® estimates that of the 45 million existing decks, only 40% are completely safe.

Because decks appear to be simple to build, many people do not realize that decks are, in fact, structures that need to be designed to adequately resist certain stresses. Like any other house or building, a deck must be designed to support the weight of people, snow loads, and objects. A deck must be able to resist lateral and uplift loads that can act on the deck as a result of wind or seismic activity. Deck stairs must be safe and handrails graspable. And, finally, deck rails should be safe for children by having proper infill spacing.

A deck failure is any failure of a deck that could lead to injury, including rail failure, or total deck collapse. There is no international system that tracks deck failures, and each is treated as an isolated event, rather than a systemic problem. Very few municipalities perform investigations into the cause of deck failures, and the media are generally more concerned with injuries than with the causes of collapses. Rail failure occurs much more frequently than total deck collapses; however, because rail failures are less dramatic than total collapses and normally don't result in death, injuries from rail failures are rarely reported.

Here are some interesting facts about deck failure:

- More decks collapse in the summer than during the rest of the year.

- Almost every deck collapse occurred while the decks were occupied or under a heavy snow load.

- There is no correlation between deck failure and whether the deck was built with or without a building permit.

- There is no correlation between deck failure and whether the deck was built by a homeowner or a professional contractor.

- There is a slight correlation between deck failure and the age of the deck.

- About 90% of deck collapses occurred as a result of the separation of the deck ledger board from the house, allowing the deck to swing away from the house. It is very rare for deck floor joists to break mid-span.

- Many more injuries are the result of rail failure, rather than complete deck collapse.

- Deck stairs are notorious for lacking graspable handrails.

- Many do-it-yourself homeowners, and even contractors, don't believe that rail infill spacing codes apply to decks.

This book does not address specific building codes, balconies, lumber species, grade marks, decks made of plastic or composites, mold, or wood-destroying insects.

This book focuses on single-level residential and commercial wood decks. The recommendations found within this publication exceed the requirements of both InterNACHI's Home Inspection Standards of Practice and the International Standards of Practice for Inspecting Commercial Properties.

A proper deck inspection relies heavily on the professional judgment of the inspector. This manual will help improve the accuracy of those judgments.

Required Deck Inspection Tools:

- flashlight;
- measuring tape;
- ladder;
- level;
- plumb bob;
- probing tool; and
- hammer.

Optional Deck Inspection Tools:

- moisture meter;
- magnet; and
- calculator.

Decks and Similar Structures

Decks Defined

Decks, porches, balconies, verandas and patios are outdoor architectural elements that are often confused with one another. An explanation of their intended use, history and design allow for useful distinctions, although a certain degree of exception and overlap is unavoidable.

A deck is a large, raised wooden floor attached to the back of a house, and contained by a perimeter railing for safety. Decks are rarely covered, and usually have a rough or informal look that is not integrated with the rest of the house's design. They are typically intended to be locations for large outdoor social gatherings. Access to the deck may be from the ground through a stairway, or from the house through a back door, or both.

Deck Facts:

- The word "deck," in this context, is generalized from decks on a ship.
- The word "deck" originates from the Middle Low German word *verdeck*, meaning covering.
- The first commercial boardwalk in the United States, which is considered a deck, was built in Atlantic City, New Jersey, and opened to the public in 1870.

Porches

A porch is a wooden structure that forms a covered entrance to a doorway at ground level. It is typically located at the front of the house, although many homes have both front and back porches.

Porch Facts:

- Porches are often used as ante-rooms where muddy or wet outerwear can be shed before entering the house.
- The word "porch" originates from the Latin word *porta*, which means gate or entrance.
- While many houses in the southern United States, as well as Victorian-style houses, have large porches suitable for social gatherings, most modern porches are too small for comfortable social use, and merely add to the visual appeal of the building.
- Porches are typically integrated with the house's architecture by using similar design elements.

Verandahs

A veranda is a long, roofed, open gallery built around a central structure and supported by pillars. Verandahs are often long enough to extend around the front and sides of a structure. Their origins are uncertain, but they are known to be a hybrid of Indian and European styles.

Verandah Facts:

- "Verandah" is alternately spelled "veranda."

- The word "verandah" appears in Hindi and several other native Indian languages, although it appears to be an adaptation of the Portuguese and Spanish *baranda*.

- Australia and New Zealand have their own unique styles of verandah. Some verandahs in these countries are roof-like structures that surround commercial buildings, often on every floor. Their purpose is to provide protection from the sun.

Balconies

A balcony is a platform that protrudes from the wall of an upper floor of a building and is enclosed by a railing. Balconies are often highly decorative, especially in wealthy and scenic areas. They are not designed as social areas but, rather, add an outdoor ambiance to the indoors.

Balcony Facts:

- In William Shakespeare's *Romeo and Juliet*, Juliet famously courted Romeo from her balcony. The small balcony design typically associated with that scene is often referred to as a "Juliet balcony."

- Balconies can be large enough to resemble decks, but they do not provide access to the ground.

- "Balcony" originates from the Italian word *balcone*, which means large window.

- Balconies are made from wood, iron, stone, and many other masonry materials.

Patios

A typical patio is a paved, roofless surface adjoining a residence that is generally intended for dining and recreation. These open-air living spaces are at ground level and are usually made from cement, stone, slate, or a combination of these materials.

Patio Facts:

- "Patio" originates from the Latin word *patere*, meaning to lie open.

- "Patio" is Spanish for backyard or back garden.

- In Australia, a patio often refers to any kind of outdoor verandah or balcony.

Quiz 1

1. A common safety issue found during a deck inspection is a lack of _____.

   ☐ guardrail infill

   ☐ soundproofing

   ☐ pavement

2. A non-graspable handrail is a(n) _____.

   ☐ optional add-on

   ☐ safety concern

   ☐ cosmetic feature

3. T/F: A deck, unlike a balcony, can be constructed as a freestanding feature of a house.

   ☐ True

   ☐ False

Answer Key is on page 38.

From the Ground Up

Deck Load

A deck inspection should progress in much the same order as deck construction. Inspectors should start at the bottom. If a deck is deemed unsafe from underneath, the inspector should not walk out onto the deck to inspect the decking, handrails, etc. The inspector should stop and report the safety issues.

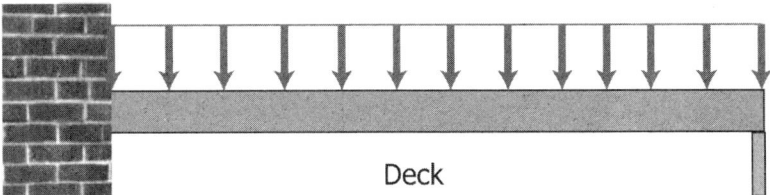

The image above depicts an evenly distributed deck load. Building codes require decks to be designed to carry a uniformly distributed load over the entire deck. If evenly distributed, half of the load is carried by the deck-to-house connection, and the other half is carried by the posts.

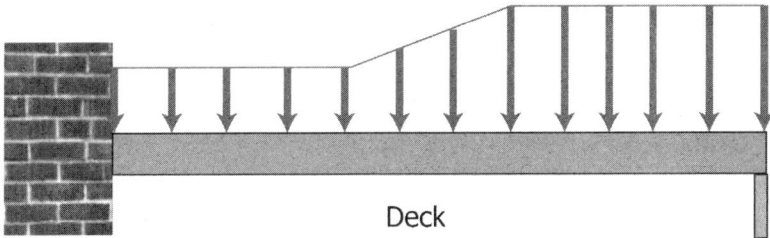

The image above depicts a typical deck load distribution. People tend to gather near the railings of a deck, so more load is likely carried by the posts.

Hot tubs filled with water and people are heavy and can weigh a couple of tons. Most decks are designed for loads of 40 to 60 pounds per square foot. Hot tubs require framing that can support more than 100 pounds per square foot.

Footings and Posts

The required depth for footings varies based on local building codes. The depth is normally below the frost line, or 12 inches in regions where frost lines are not applicable.

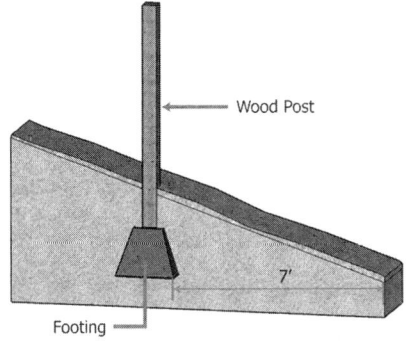

The image to the left depicts the "7-Foot Rule." On steep properties, the slope of the ground around the footing could affect the footing's stability. The 7-Foot Rule states that there should be a least 7 feet between the bottom of a footing and daylight.

Posts in contact with soil should be pressure-treated and oriented so the cut end is above grade.

The image at right shows a freestanding deck (not attached to the home or building). The footing near the home should not be placed in disturbed soil. Disturbed soils are those which have been altered as a result of grading or construction, etc., giving the soil variable characteristics. Some codes consider soil to be "undisturbed" if it hasn't been disturbed in more than five years. The inspector may discover that, because of its location, a footing near the home was not properly placed in undisturbed soil. A footing placed in undisturbed soil is desirable because that soil is more compacted and solid. Placing a footing in disturbed soil is less stable and may result in incremental failure of the deck's support, as the footing is likely to sink lower and lower into the poorly bearing soil.

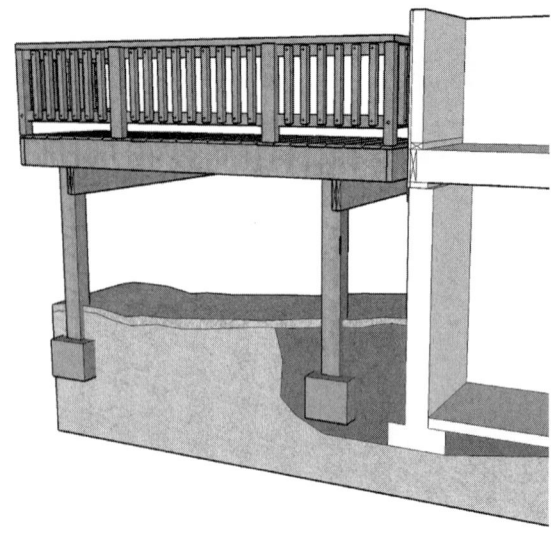

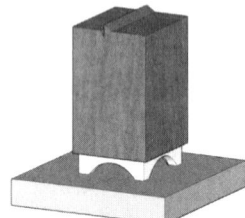

The image at left depicts a post base that is not attached to its footing. Posts should be connected to their footings so that the posts don't lift or slip off.

The image at right depicts a pre-cast concrete pier. Posts can lift out of pre-cast concrete piers, and piers can slide. Posts should be connected to their footings so that the posts don't lift or slip off.

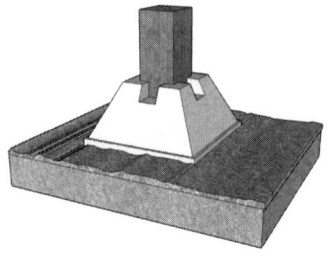

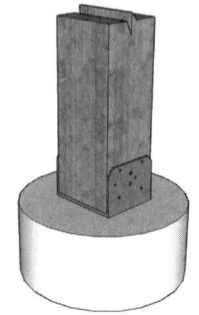

The image at left depicts a proper post-to-footing connection. Posts should be connected to their footings so that the posts don't lift or slip off their footings.

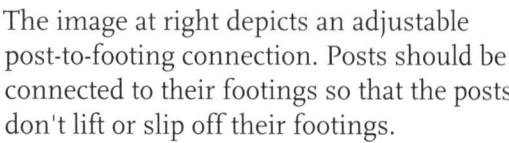

The image at right depicts an adjustable post-to-footing connection. Posts should be connected to their footings so that the posts don't lift or slip off their footings.

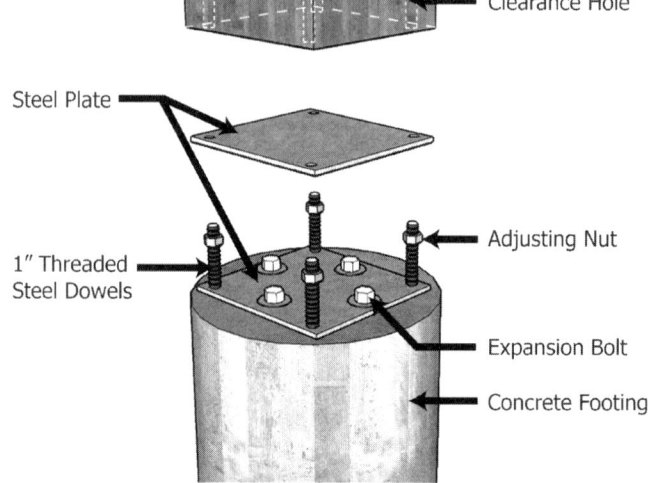

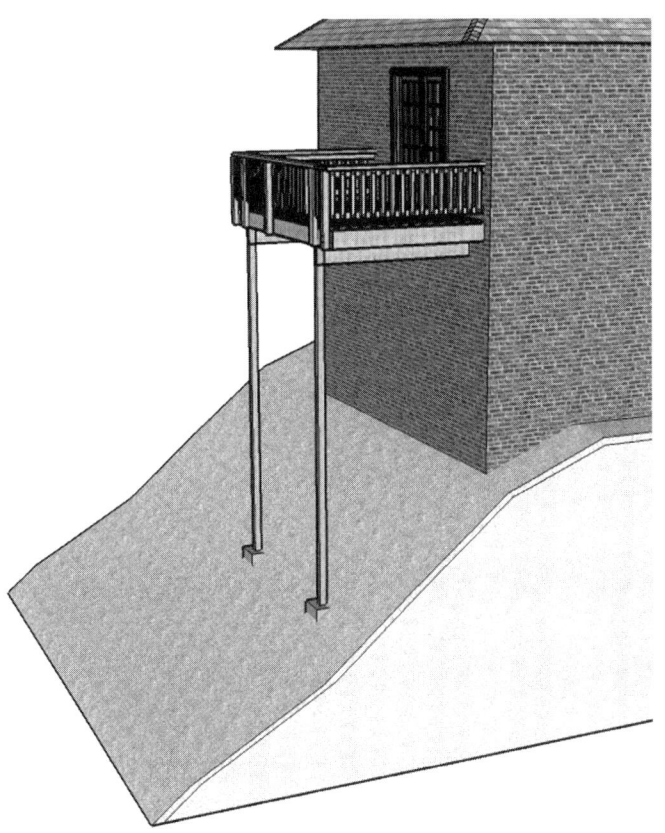

The image at left depicts a high deck being supported with 4x4-inch posts. Tall 4x4-inch posts twist under load, and 4x4-inch posts, even when treated, decay below grade too quickly. In all but the lowest of decks, deck posts should be at least 6x6 inches and be no higher than 12 feet; 14 feet is acceptable if cross-bracing is used.

Often, the bottoms of the stringer boards for deck stairs have been found to rest on soil, concrete block or rock, as opposed to resting on posts installed below the frost line. Posts set on soil are subject to rot due to moisture. Posts that are set in unsound footings may cause movement and make the deck above unstable.

Quiz 2

1. T/F: Most people congregate on decks near railings, so the deck load is often unevenly distributed.

   ☐ True

   ☐ False

2. The "7-Foot Rule" states that there should be at least 7 feet between _____.

   ☐ the top of the stairs and the ground

   ☐ the bottom of the footing and daylight

   ☐ each supporting post

3. Posts in contact with soil should be _____.

   ☐ sanded well

   ☐ pressure-treated

   ☐ heavily varnished

4. T/F: Posts should be connected to their footings so that the posts don't lift out or slip off.

   ☐ True

   ☐ False

Answer Key is on page 38.

Wood Decay

Moisture and Wood Decay

The image at right depicts a lawn sprinkler keeping a deck post wet. Lawn sprinkler systems that regularly keep the deck wet contribute to decay.

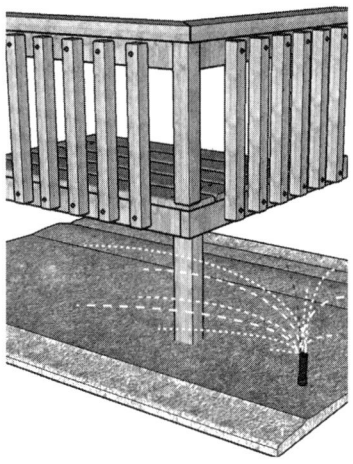

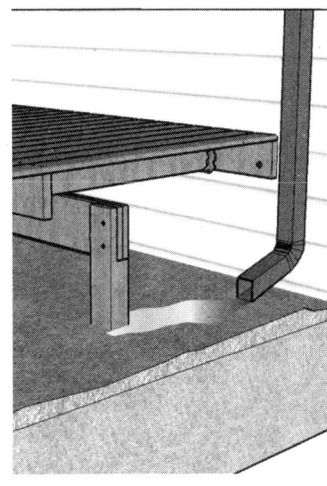

The image at left depicts a downspout contributing to post decay. Downspouts should not discharge near deck posts.

The image at right depicts the indentation left over from the footing hole, causing a puddle. Puddles contribute to post decay.

Wood can decay and degrade over time with exposure to the elements. Decay is a problem that worsens with time. Members within the deck frame that have decayed may no longer be able to perform the function for which they were installed. Paint can hide decay from an inspector and so should be noted in the report.

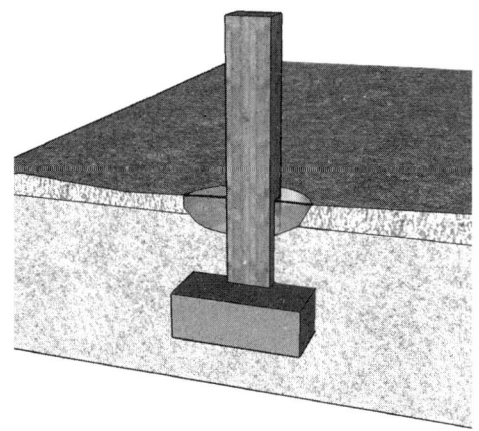

The Pick Test

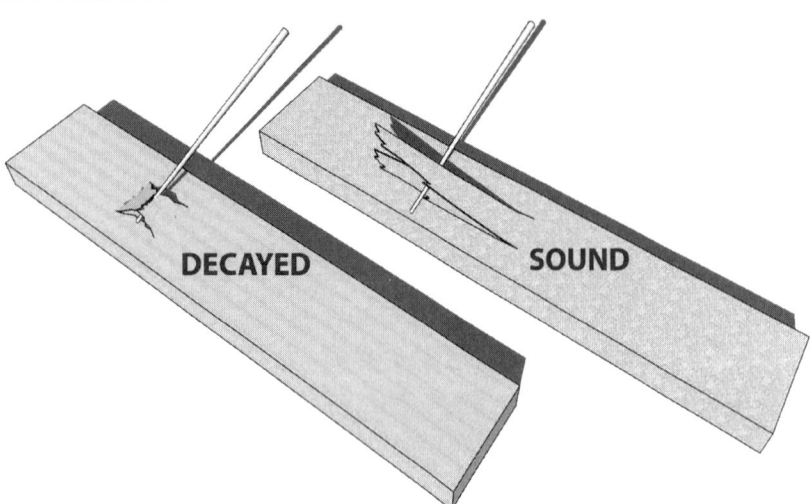

DECAYED   SOUND

The image at left depicts a "pick test." The pick test uses an ice pick, awl or screwdriver to penetrate the wood surface. After penetrating the wood, the tool is leveraged to pry up a splinter parallel to the grain and away from the surface. The appearance and sound of the action is used to detect decay. The inspector should first try the pick test in an area where the wood is known to be sound to determine a control for the rest of the inspection. Decayed wood will break directly over the tool with very few splinters and little or almost no audible noise compared to sound wood. The pick test cannot detect decay far from the surface of the wood.

The image at right depicts a pick test on a deck post. Although deck inspections are visual-only inspections, inspectors may want to dig down around posts and perform pick tests just below grade level to look for decay.

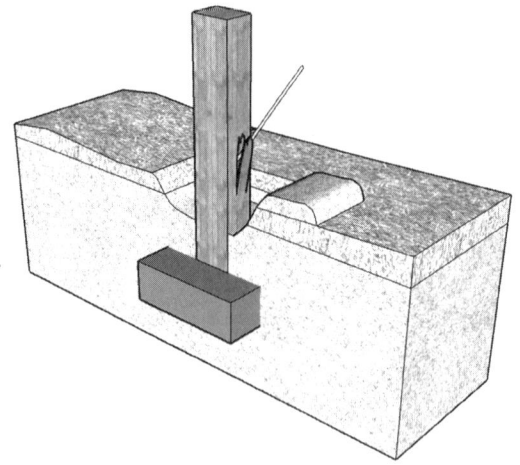

Quiz 3

1. Painting deck posts can _____ wood decay.

      ☐ repair

      ☐ cause

      ☐ hide

2. T/F: Using the pick test, decayed wood will pull away with a lot of splinters.

      ☐ True

      ☐ False

3. T/F: Using the pick test, structurally sound wood will make almost no noise.

      ☐ True

      ☐ False

Answer Key is on page 38.

Supports and Connections

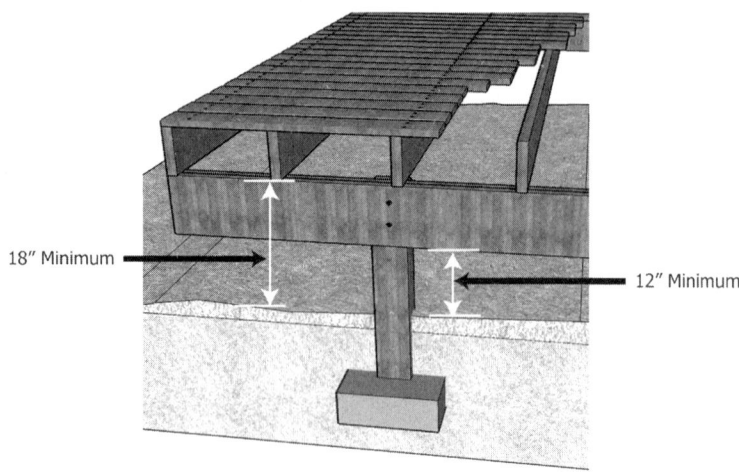

18" Minimum

12" Minimum

Girders and Beams

The image at left depicts the minimum distance of untreated support members from grade. Untreated joists should be at least 18 inches away from the ground. Girders should be 12 inches away from the ground. However, in many situations, exceptions are made where the elevation of the home does not provide for these minimum distances and the climate is very dry.

The image at right depicts a girder improperly relying on the shear strength of lag bolts. Girders should bear directly on posts.

The image at left depicts a girder properly resting on a notched post. Girders should bear directly on posts.

The image at right depicts a girder properly resting on a post. Girders should bear directly on posts.

Girders supporting joists should not be supported by deck ledgers or band joists.

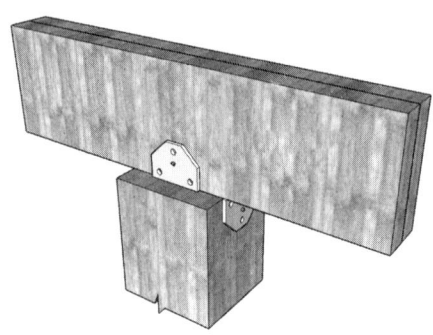

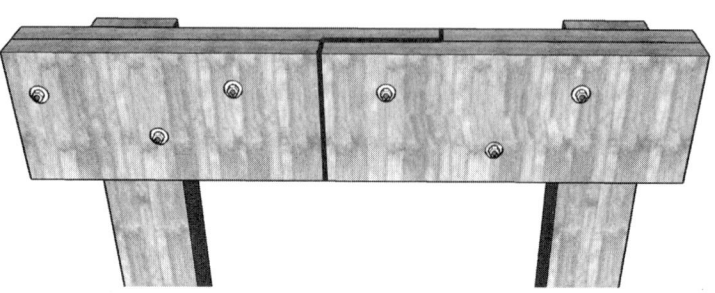

The image at left depicts a butt joint improperly located within a girder span. Butt joints in a girder span are generally not permitted unless specially engineered. Butt joints typically must be located above posts.

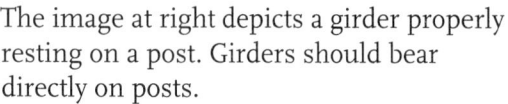

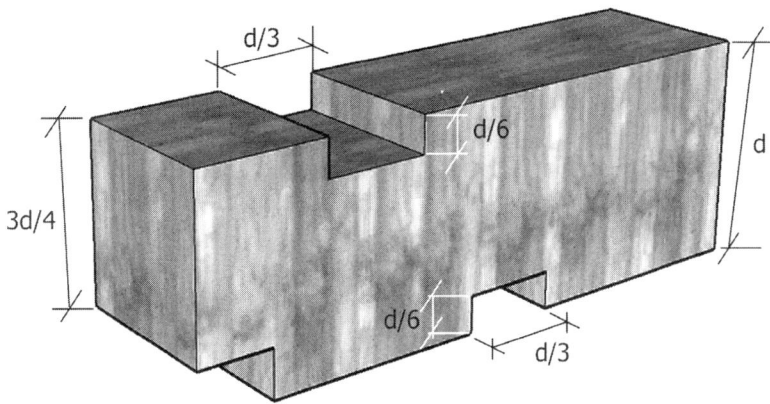

The image above depicts notches in a supporting beam. Notches must be less than one-quarter the depth of the member. On the tension and compression faces, the notch depth must be less than one-sixth of the member's depth, and the notch length must be less than one-third of the member's depth. Notches are not permitted in the middle third of spans, or on the tension face of members that are greater than 3-1/2 inches thick.

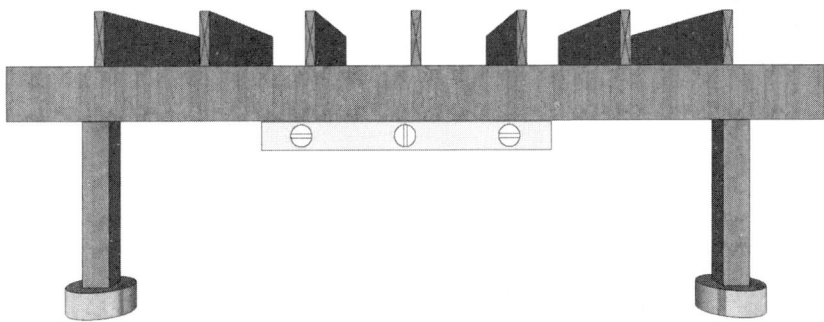

The image above depicts a level being used to check for beam sag. Even with a carpenter's level, it can be difficult to see beam sag from the front.

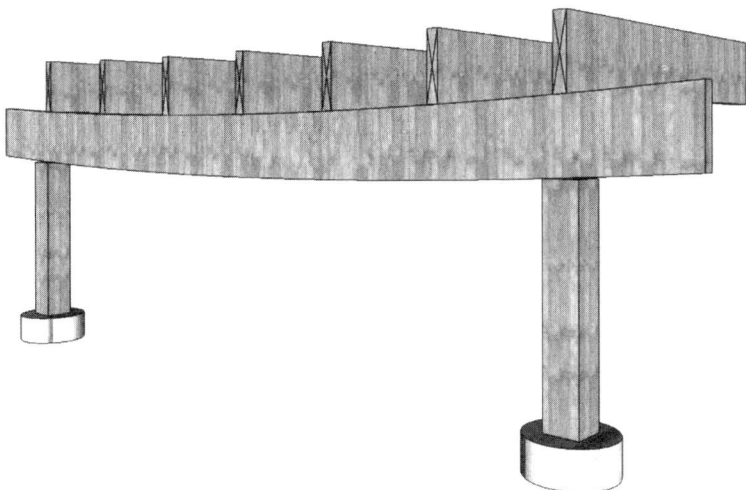

The image above depicts beam sag being eyed-up. It is often easier to detect beam sag by eye than with a level by looking along the bottom edge of the beam.

Ledger Connections

The most common cause of deck collapse is when a ledger pulls away from the band joists of the home or building.

The two most common ways to correctly attach a ledger to a structure are with lag screws or through-bolts. The installation of through-bolts requires access to the backside of the rim joist, which, in some cases, is not possible without significant removal of drywall within the structure.

Most building codes state that where positive connections to the primary building structure cannot be verified during inspection, decks shall be self-supporting (freestanding).

Determining the exact required spacing for the ledger fasteners is based on many factors, including:

- joist length;
- type of fastener;
- diameter of fastener;
- sheathing thickness;
- use of stacked washers;
- type of wood species;
- moisture content;
- band joist integrity; and
- deck loads...

...and so is beyond the scope of a visual inspection. However, the spacing of ledger fasteners required is primarily determined by the length of the joists.

InterNACHI's ledger-fastener spacing formula provides inspectors with this rule of thumb:

On-center spacing of ledger fasteners in inches = 100 ÷ joist length in feet.

A deck with substantially fewer ledger fasteners than that recommended by InterNACHI's formula may be unsafe.

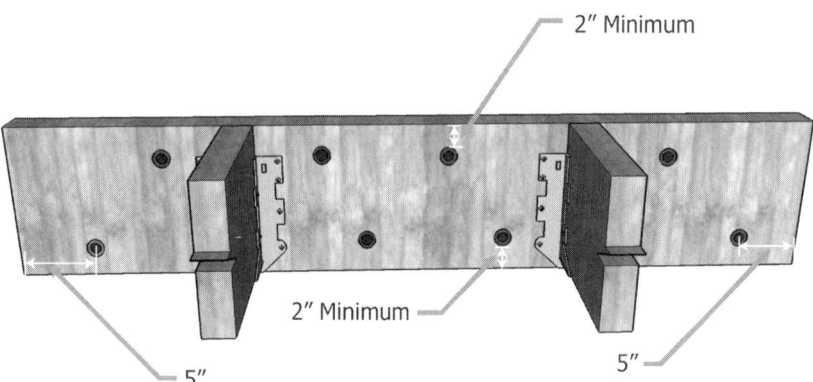

The image above shows the minimum distance of fasteners to the edges and ends of a ledger board. Lag screws or bolts should be staggered vertically, placed at least 2 inches from the bottom or top and 5 inches from the ends of the ledger board. Some codes permit the lag screws or bolts to be as close as 2 inches from the ends of the ledger board; however, avoiding the very ends of the ledger boards minimizes splitting from load stress.

Through-bolts should be a minimum of 1/2-inch in diameter and have washers at the bolt head and nut. Lag screws should also be a minimum of 1/2-inch in diameter and have washers. Expansion and adhesive anchors should also have washers.

Deck ledgers should be made of at least 2x8 pressure-treated wood.

There are three ways a joist can be attached to a ledger:

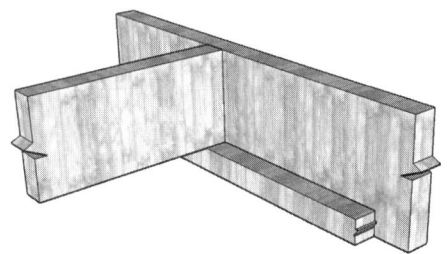

The first is by resting the joist on a ledger strip. The image at left depicts a joist properly resting on a 2x2-inch ledger strip.

The second is by notching over a ledger strip. The image at right depicts a notched joist properly resting a 2x2-inch ledger strip.

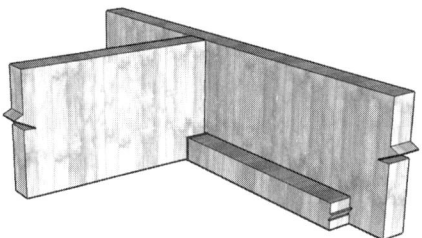

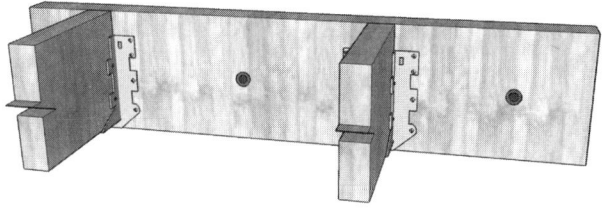

The third is by hanging the joists with joist hangers. The image at left depicts joists properly attached to a ledger using metal joist hangers.

The image at right depicts a joist cut too short. Joists may rest on 2x2-inch ledgers like the one above (or in joist hangers), but joists must be cut long enough to reach the ledger or band joist that is supporting them.

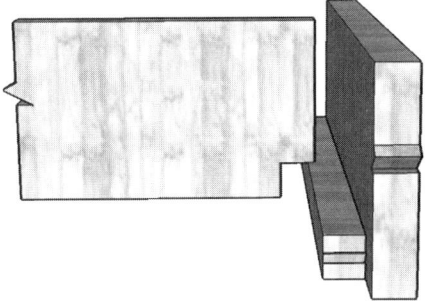

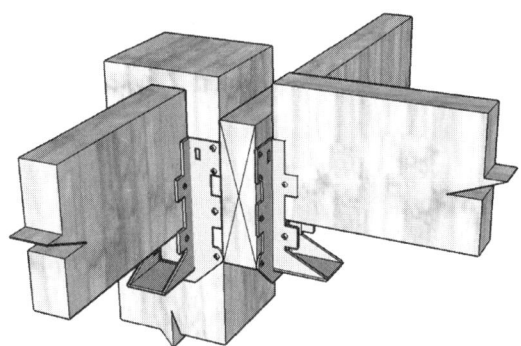

The image at left depicts joists that are not fully resting in their joist hangers. Joists should be fully resting in their joist hangers.

Ledger Board and Band Joist Contact

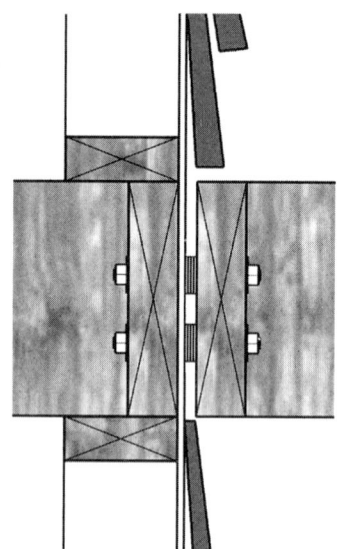

The image at right depicts washers being used as spacers between the ledger board and band joist, which is incorrect.

In some cases, the ledger board and band joist are intentionally kept separated by a stack of washers on the lag screw or bolts to allow water to run between the two boards. In other cases, there is insulation between the two boards. Even worse is when the siding or exterior finish system was not removed prior to the installation of the ledger board. Situations like these, where the ledger board and band joist are not in direct contact, significantly reduce the strength of the ledger connection to the structure and are not recommended by InterNACHI®, unless the two members are sandwiching structural sheathing.

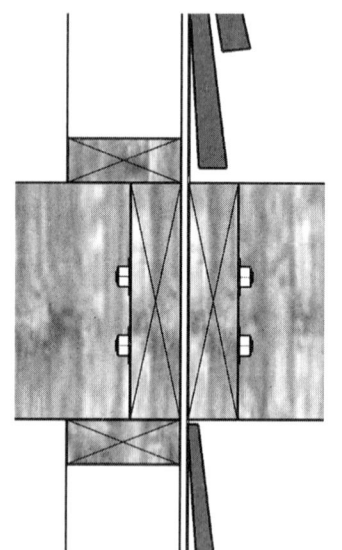

The image at left depicts a ledger board and band joist sandwiching the structural sheathing (correct).

All through-bolts should have washers at the bolt head and nut.

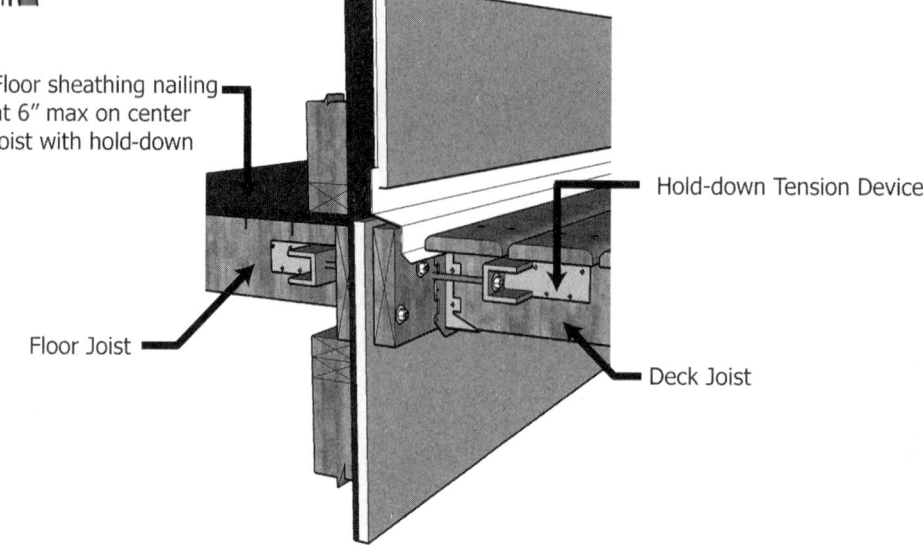

Floor sheathing nailing at 6" max on center joist with hold-down

Hold-down Tension Device

Floor Joist

Deck Joist

The image above depicts a hold-down tension device. The *2007 IRC Supplement* requires hold-down tension devices at no fewer than two locations per deck.

Codes in some areas outright forbid attaching a ledger board to an open-web floor truss.

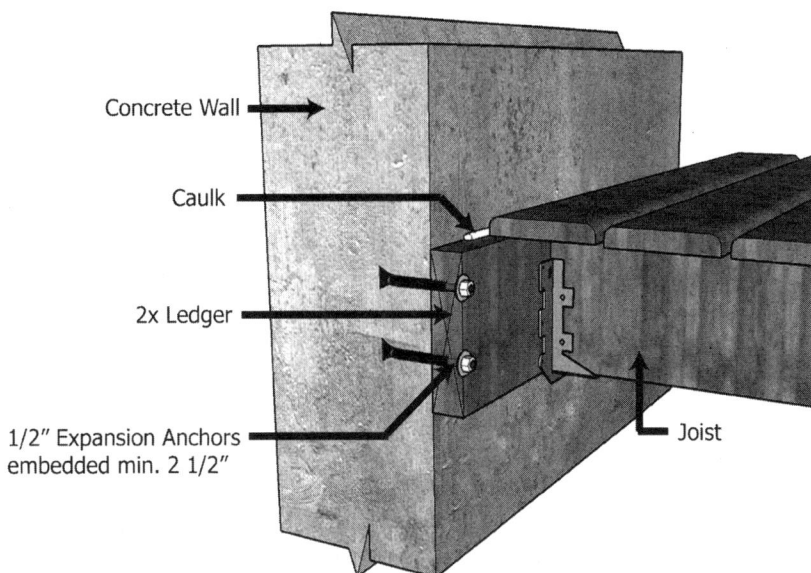

Concrete Wall

Caulk

2x Ledger

1/2" Expansion Anchors
embedded min. 2 1/2"

Joist

The image at left depicts
a ledger board attached to
a concrete wall. Caulking
rather than flashing is used.

The image at right depicts a
ledger board attached to hollow
masonry. When the ledger is
attached to a hollow masonry
wall, the cell should be grouted.

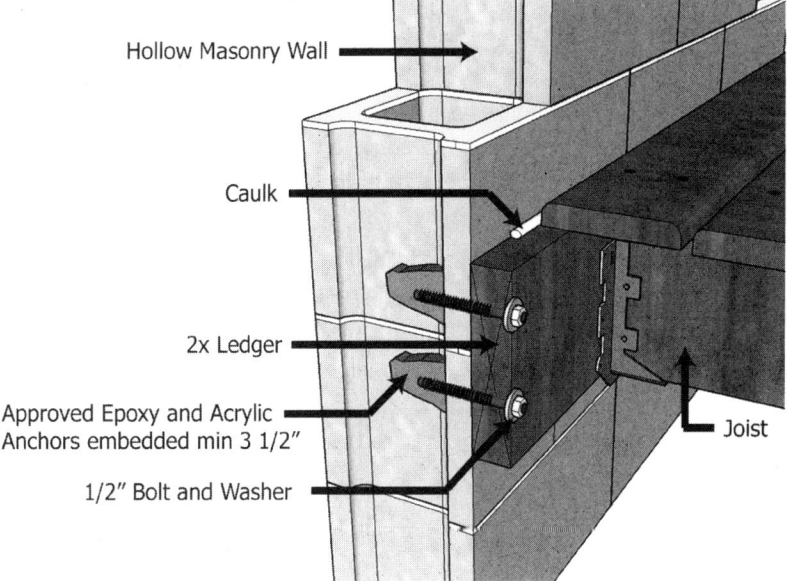

Hollow Masonry Wall

Caulk

2x Ledger

Approved Epoxy and Acrylic
Anchors embedded min 3 1/2"

1/2" Bolt and Washer

Joist

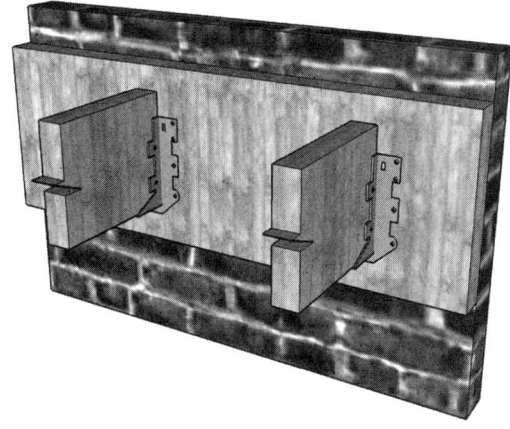

The image at left depicts a ledger board improperly
supported by brick veneer. Ledger boards should not be
supported by stone or brick veneer.

Ledger boards should not be attached directly (surface-
mounted) to stucco or EIFS, either. Stucco and EIFS
have to be cut back so that ledger boards can be
attached directly to band joists; however, cut-back
stucco and EIFS are difficult to flash and weather-proof.

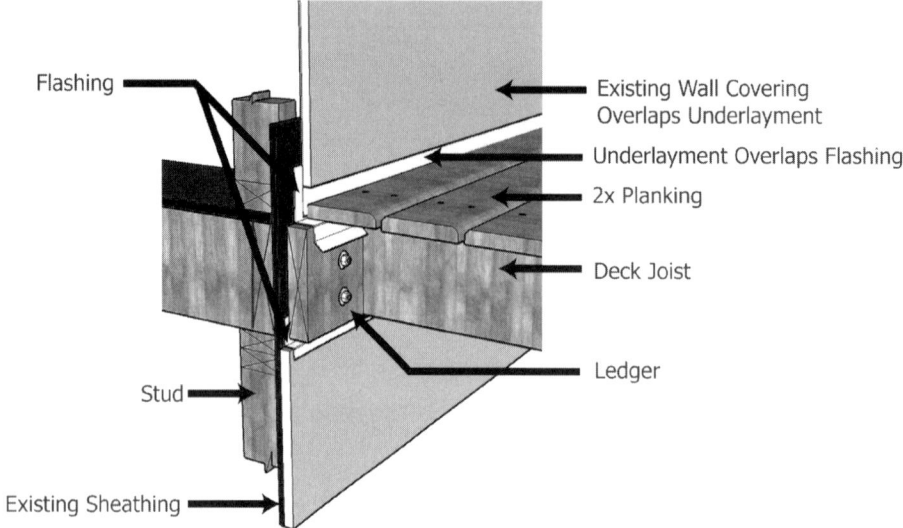

The image above depicts flashing at both over and under the ledger board. The ledger board should always be flashed even when the home or building has a protective roof overhang.

Aluminum flashing is commonly available but should not be used. Contact with pressure-treated wood or galvanized fasteners can lead to rapid corrosion of the aluminum.

Overhangs

The image at right depicts a deck ledger attached to an overhang. Decks should not be attached to overhangs.

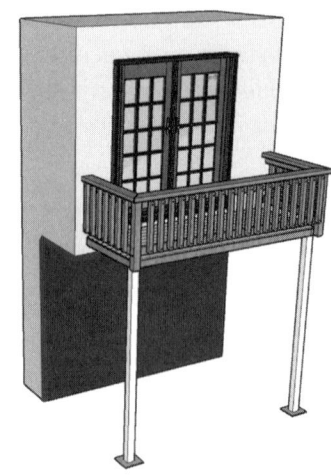

Framing Around

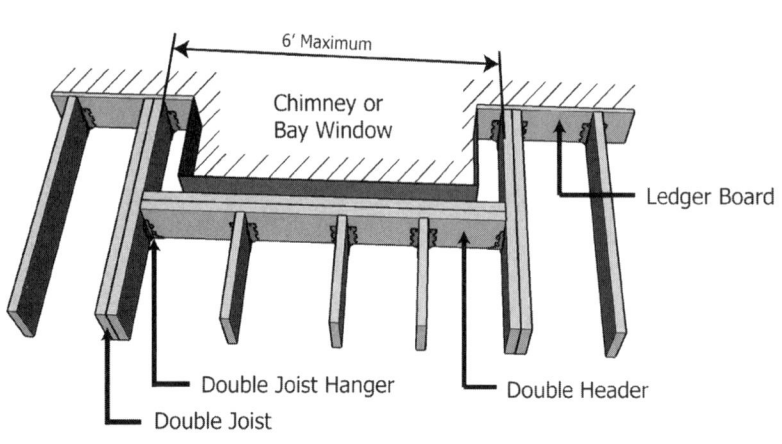

The image at left depicts proper framing for around chimneys and bay windows that are up to 6 feet wide.

Framing around chimneys and bay windows that are more than 6 feet wide requires additional posts.

Cantilevered Decks

The image at right depicts a cantilevered deck. Joists should be cantilevered no more than one-quarter of the joist length and three times the joist width (nominal depth). Both conditions must be true.

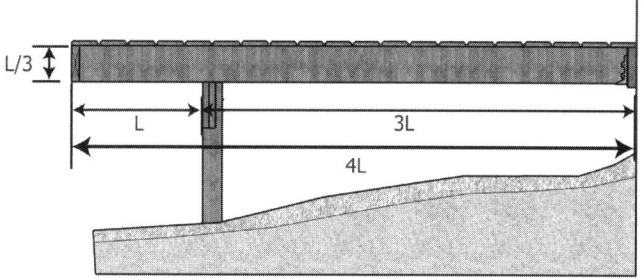

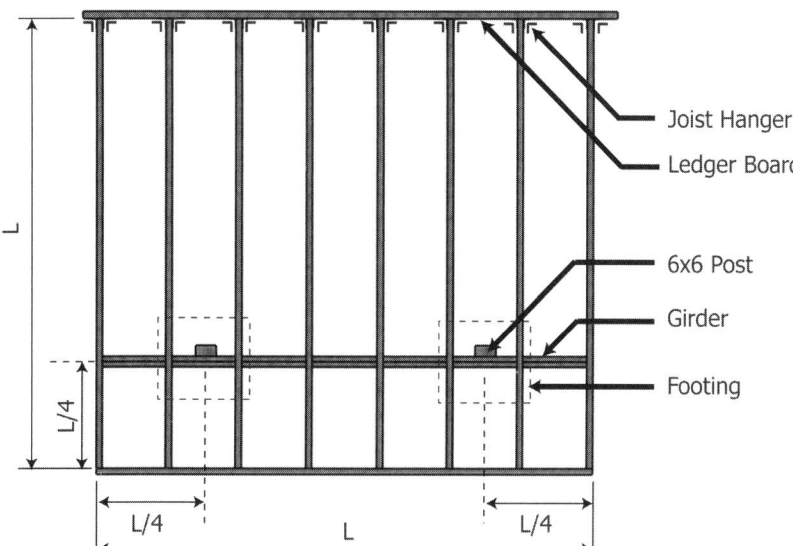

Joist Hanger

Ledger Board

6x6 Post

Girder

Footing

The image at left depicts a joist cantilever in the front of the deck and girder cantilevers on both sides of deck posts. Joists should be cantilevered no more than one-quarter the joist length and three times the joist width (nominal depth). Girders can be cantilevered over their posts no more than one-quarter the girder length.

Bracing

The image at right depicts a deck with post-to-joist diagonal bracing. Decks greater than 6 feet above grade should have diagonal bracing from posts to girder and from posts to joists.

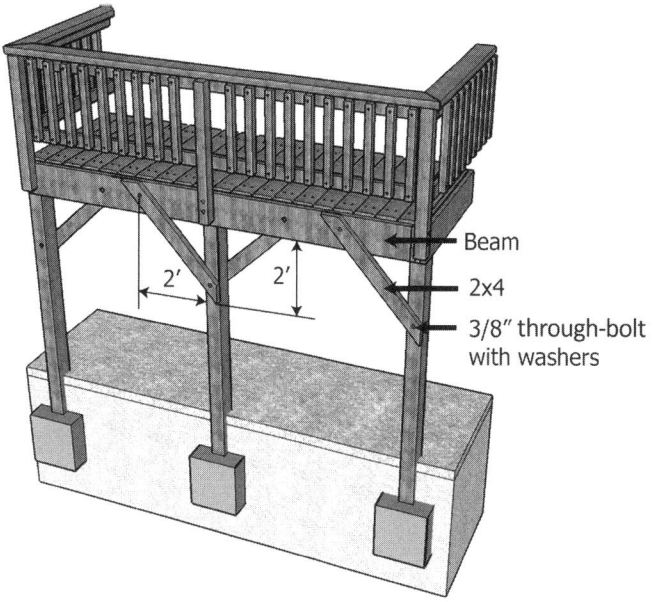

Beam

2x4

3/8″ through-bolt with washers

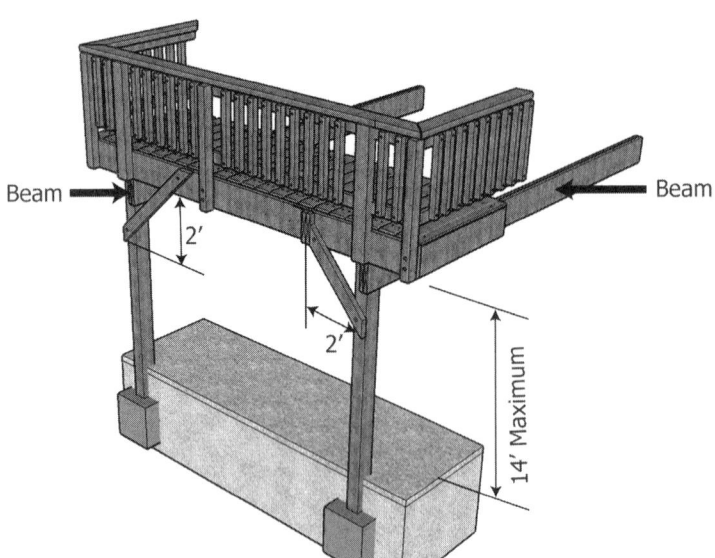

Beam

Beam

2'

2'

14' Maximum

The image at left depicts a deck with post-to-girder diagonal bracing. Decks greater than 6 feet above grade should have diagonal bracing from posts to girder and from posts to joists.

Freestanding decks (not supported by the home or building) should have diagonal bracing on all sides.

The image at right depicts underside diagonal bracing of a deck. Decks greater than 6 feet above grade that do not have diagonal decking should have diagonal bracing across the bottoms of the joists to keep the deck square. A deck that is not held square could permit the outer posts to lean to the right or left, parallel to the ledger board, and thus twist the ledger away from the home or building.

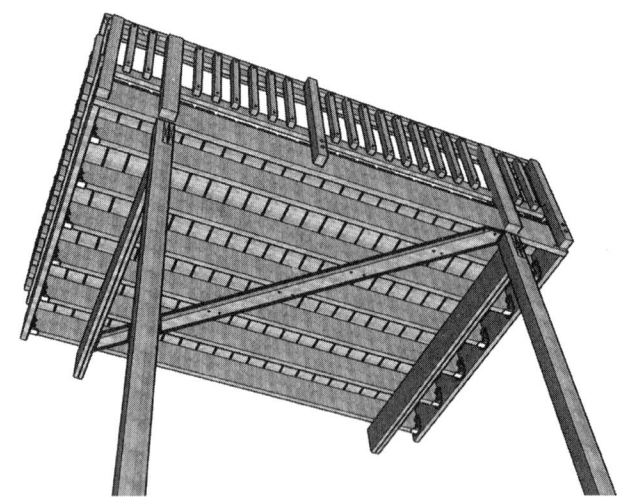

Connectors and Fasteners

The inspector should note missing connectors or fasteners. All lag screws and bolts should have washers.

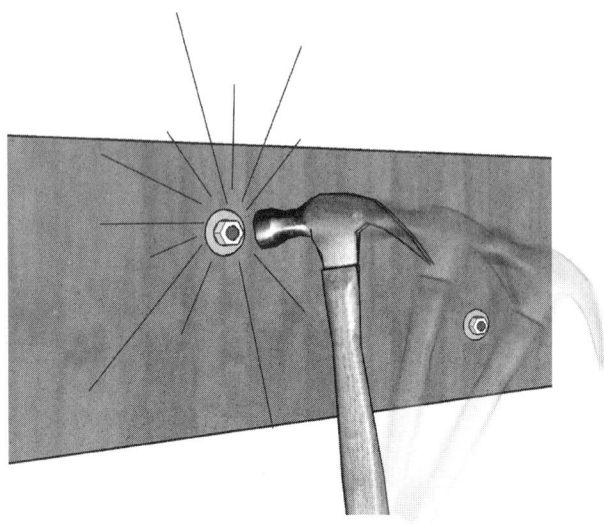

The image at left depicts a "hammer test." Depending on how the deck was built, vital connections may have degraded over time due to various factors. Issues such as wobbly railings, loose stairs, and ledgers that appear to be pulling away from the adjacent structure are all causes for concern. The tightness of fasteners should be checked. If it is not possible to reach both sides of a bolt, it may be struck with a hammer. The ring will sound hollow with vibration if the fastener is loose. The ring will sound solid if the connection is tight. The hammer test is subjective, so the inspector should hammer-test bolts that can be confirmed as tight or loose, and compare the sounds of the rings to develop a control.

Corrosion of Connectors and Fasteners

All screws, bolts and nails should be hot-dipped galvanized, stainless steel, silicon bronze, copper, zinc-coated, or corrosion-resistant. Metal connectors and fasteners can corrode over time, especially if a product with insufficient corrosion resistance was originally installed. Corrosion of a fastener affects both the fastener and the wood. As the fastener corrodes, it causes the wood around it to deteriorate. As the fastener becomes smaller, the void around it becomes larger. Inspectors normally do not remove fasteners to check their quality or size, but if the inspector removes a fastener, he should make sure that removal doesn't result in a safety issue. Fasteners that are removed should be from areas that have the greatest exposure to weather. Some inspectors carry new fasteners to replace ones they remove at the inspection.

Cracks

As wood ages, it is common for cracks to develop. Large cracks (longer than the depth of the member) or excessive cracking overall can weaken deck framing. Toe-nailed connections are always at risk for splitting. Splitting of lumber near connections should be noted by the inspector.

Quiz 4

1. T/F: Girders should bear directly on posts.

     ☐ True

     ☐ False

2. A "hammer test" checks for _____.

     ☐ loose fasteners

     ☐ how solid the wood is

     ☐ the strength of the hammer

3. T/F: Ledger boards can be adequately supported by stucco or brick veneer.

     ☐ True

     ☐ False

Answer Key is on page 38.

Posts and Rails

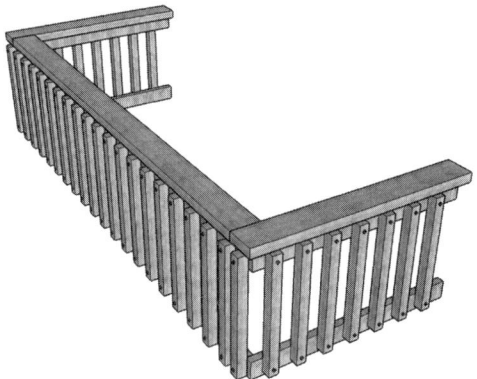

The image at left shows a guardrail supported solely by balusters. Guardrails should be supported by posts every 6 feet.

The image at right depicts a notched-deck guardrail post attachment. This common notched-type of attachment is permitted by most codes but could become unsafe, especially as the deck ages. Because of leverage, a 200-pound force pushing the deck's guardrail outward causes a 1,700-pound force at the upper bolt attaching the post. It is difficult to attach deck guardrail posts in a manner that is strong enough without using deck guardrail post brackets.

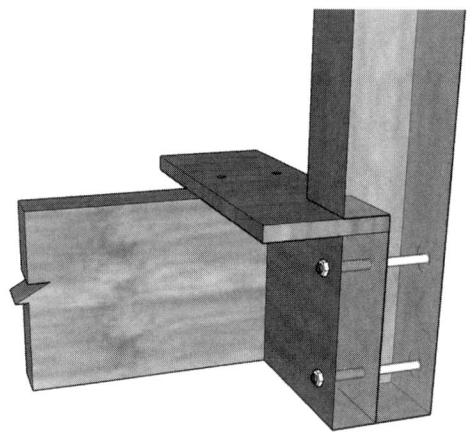

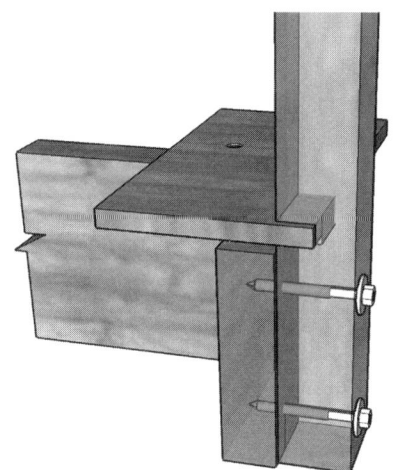

The image at left depicts a notched-deck guardrail post attachment. This notched-around-decking type of attachment is permitted by most codes but could become unsafe, especially as the deck ages. Because of leverage, a 200-pound force pushing the deck's guardrail outward causes a 1,700-pound force at the upper bolt attaching the post. It is difficult to attach deck guardrail posts in a manner that is strong enough without using deck guardrail post brackets.

The image at right depicts a deck guardrail post properly attached with brackets. Because of leverage, a 200-pound force pushing the deck's guardrail outward causes a 1,700-pound force at the upper bolt attaching the post. It is difficult to attach deck guardrail posts in a manner that is strong enough without using deck guardrail post brackets.

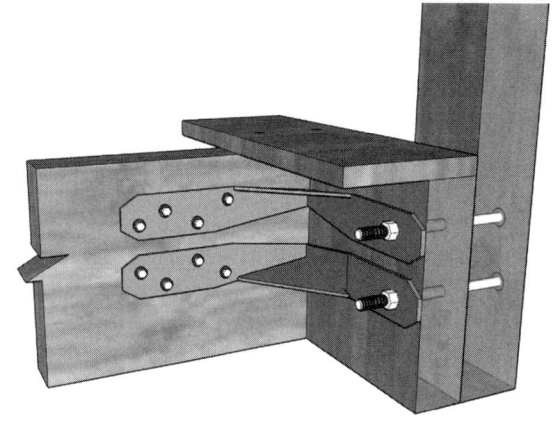

The image above-left depicts a post and balusters cut level and not shedding water. The end-grain of vertical posts and balusters should not be cut level.

The image above-right depicts a post and balusters properly cut at angles to shed water. The end-grain of vertical posts and balusters should be cut at an angle.

Missing Guardrails

Decks that are greater than 12 inches above adjacent areas should have guardrails around the edges. Some codes require guardrails only around the edges of decks 30 inches or higher.

Improper Guardrail Height

Most residential codes require the top of the guardrail to be at least 36 inches from the deck surface. Most commercial code height is 42 inches.

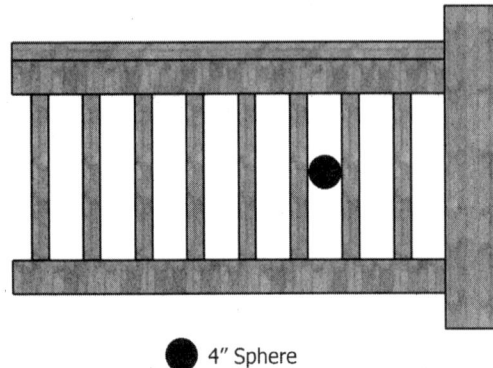

The image at left depicts guardrail infill that poses a safety hazard to children. Infill should not permit a 4-inch sphere to pass through.

4" Sphere

The image at right depicts horizontal balustrades. Ladder-type guardrail infill on high decks is prohibited by some local codes because they are easy for children to climb over.

Decking

Board Placement and Support

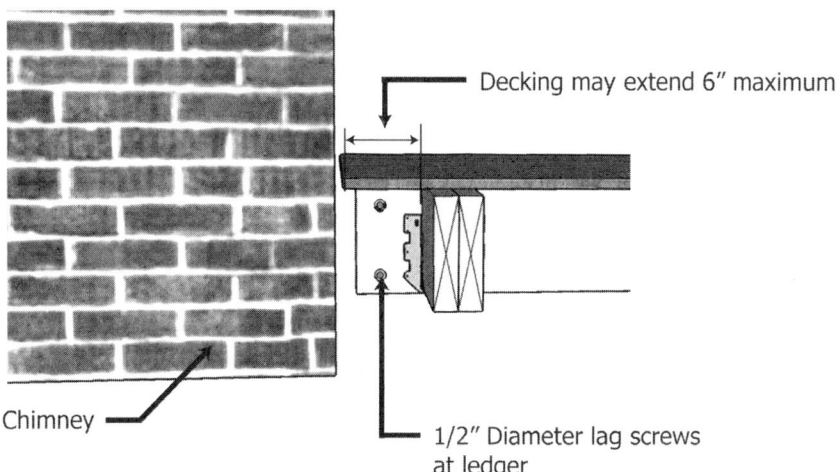

Decking may extend 6" maximum

Chimney

1/2" Diameter lag screws at ledger

The image at left depicts deck framing near a chimney or bay window. The ends of decking boards near the chimney or bay window can extend unsupported up to 6 inches.

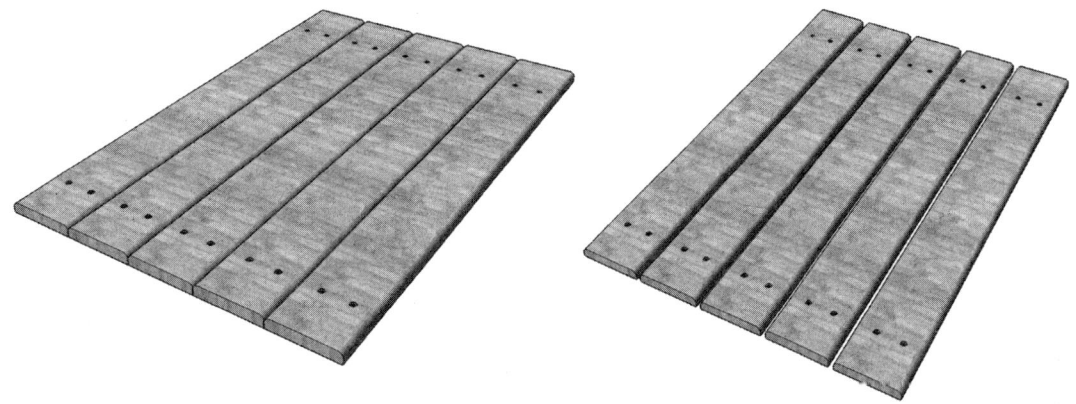

The image above-left depicts decking that is laid too tight. Decking should have 1/8-inch gaps between boards so that puddles don't form.

The image above-right depicts decking that is properly spaced. Decking should have 1/8-inch gaps between boards so that puddles don't form.

The image at right depicts decking that isn't staggered properly. Decking should be staggered so that butt joints don't land on the same joist side by side.

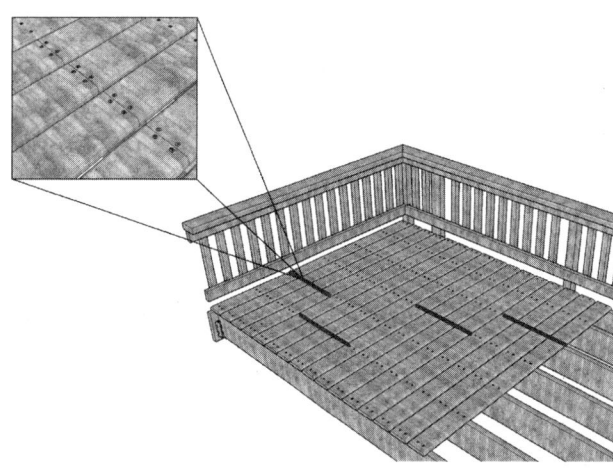

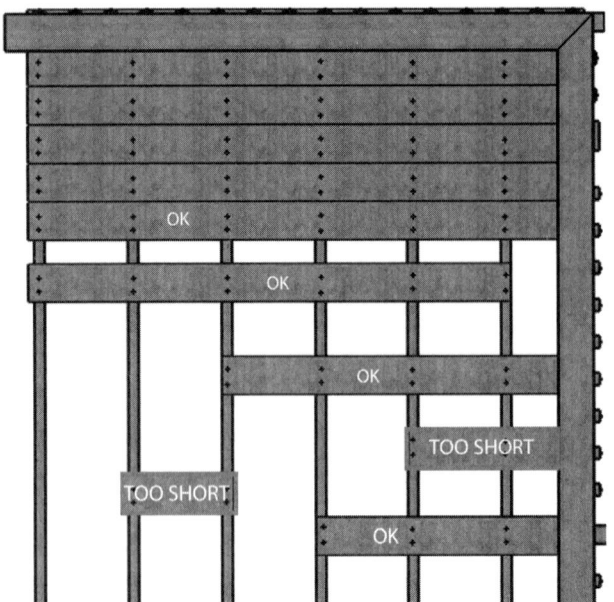

The image at left depicts decking lengths. Some are too short. Each segment of decking should bear on a minimum of four joists.

Decking should be attached to the floor joists and rim joist, especially in high-wind areas.

Decking Nail Pull-Out

Inspectors should look for splitting and nail pull-out in decking. Aside from the structural issue, nails that have pulled out or screws that are not fully driven into the decking can cause injury to bare feet and pose a tripping hazard.

Stairs

Stringers, Risers and Treads

The image at right depicts a deck stair stringer. Stair stringers shall be made of 2x12-inch lumber at a minimum, and no less than 5 inches wide at any point.

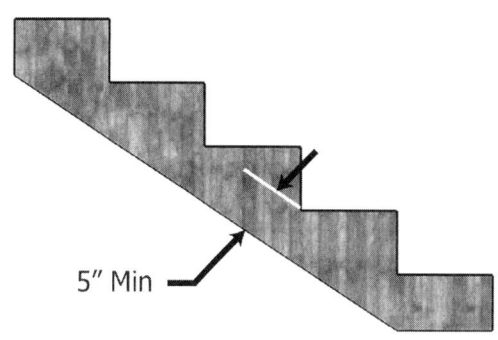

5″ Min

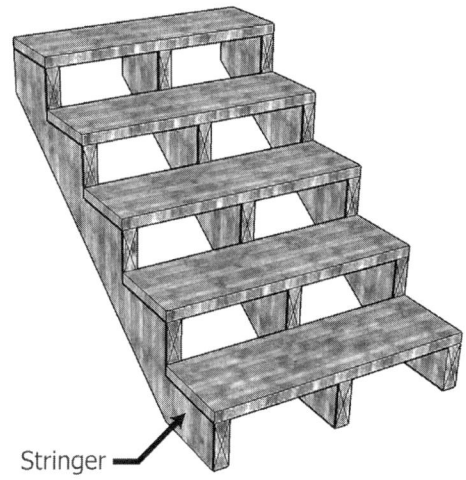

Stringer

The image at left depicts deck stair stringers. Stringers should be no more than 36 inches apart.

The image at right depicts ledger strips properly located under stair treads. Where solid stringers are used, stair treads should be supported with ledger strips (as depicted), mortised, or supported with metal brackets.

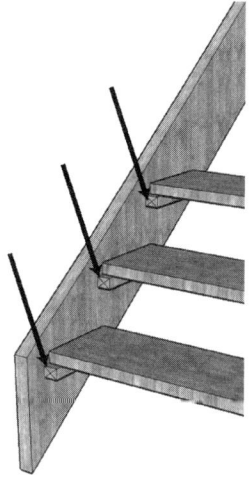

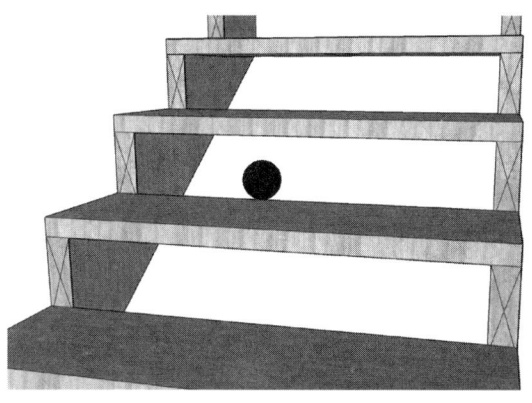

4″ Sphere

The image at left depicts a set of stairs with open risers. Most deck stairs have open risers and are not safe for children. Risers may be open but should not allow the passage of a 4-inch-diameter sphere.

The image at right depicts stair riser height. To minimize tripping, the maximum variation among riser heights (the difference between the tallest and shortest risers) should be no more than 3/8-inch.

The bottom step of a stairway leading up to a deck is typically at a different height than the rest of the steps. This can pose a tripping hazard.

Steps with open risers can present a tripping hazard if a user catches his foot by stepping too far into the tread. To mitigate this hazard, the risers can be closed or the treads can be made deeper.

Lighting

Decks rarely have light sources that cover the entire stairway. Any unlit stairway is a safety issue.

Handrails

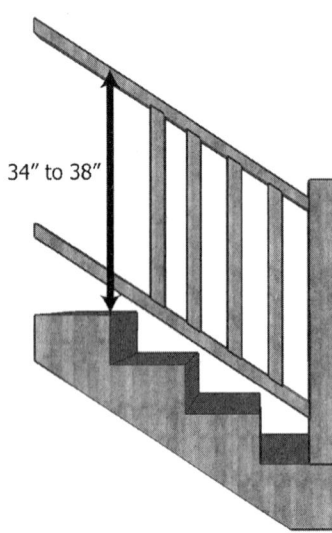

34" to 38"

Stairs with four or more risers should have a handrail on at least one side. According to the International Standards of Practice for Inspecting Commercial Properties, ramps longer than 6 feet should have handrails on both sides.

The image at left depicts proper stair handrail height. Handrail height should be between 34 and 38 inches measured vertically from the sloped plane adjoining the tread nosing.

The image at right depicts a stair handrail that is not graspable. Many deck handrails improperly consist of 2x6-inch lumber or decking. Handrails should be graspable, continuous and smooth.

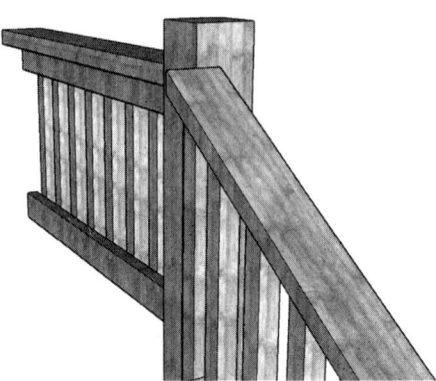

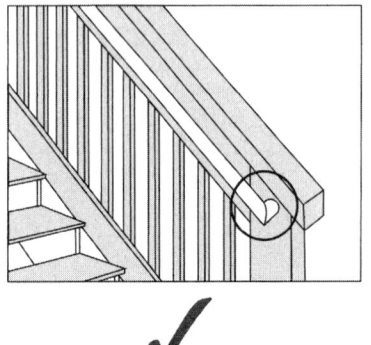

The images at left show that handrail ends should be returned or terminate in newel posts.

These three images depict graspable handrails:

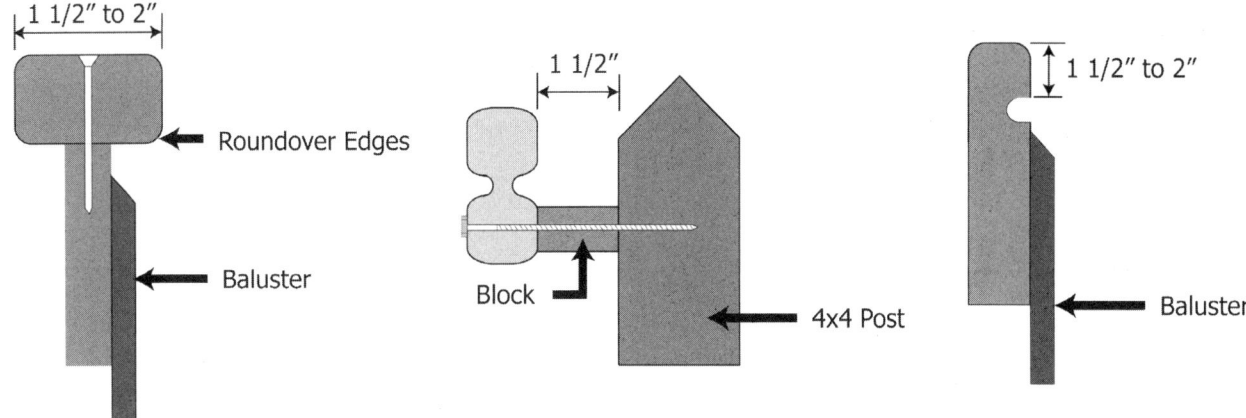

Many deck handrails improperly consist of 2x6-inch lumber or decking. Again, handrails should be graspable, continuous and smooth.

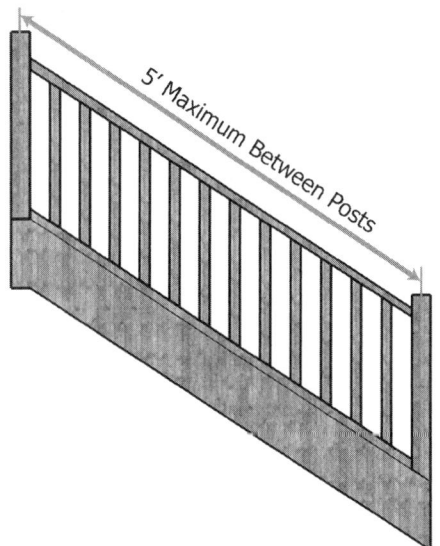

The image at left depicts the maximum distance between stair handrail posts. Stair handrails should have posts, at most, every 5 feet.

The image at right depicts permitted spacing at stairs. Larger spacing presents a child-safety issue.

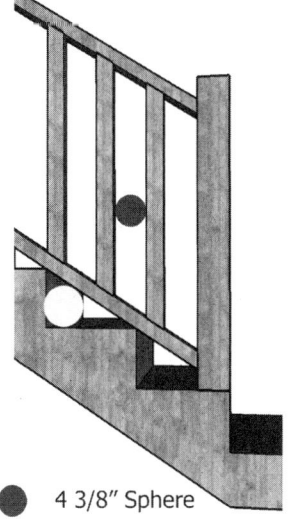

Electrical Receptacles

Receptacle Requirements

Are exterior receptacles required at decks? The 2008 edition of the *National Electrical Code* (NEC) describes two requirements for locations of outdoor receptacles in one- and two-family dwellings. The previous edition (2005) includes only one of these requirements, and inspectors should be aware of this change and understand the reason it was made. The NEC also describes how to achieve adequate weather protection for exterior receptacles.

Two Requirements for Locations of Outdoor Receptacles:

1. As of 2005, the NEC required at least one outdoor receptacle in the front and the rear of the house, and not more than 6-1/2 feet from the ground.

2. As of 2008, the NEC added the following requirement:

    Balconies, decks and porches that are accessible from inside the dwelling unit shall have at least one receptacle outlet installed within the perimeter of the balcony, deck or porch. The receptacle shall not be located more than 6-1/2 feet (2 m) above the balcony, deck or porch surface.

The code offers the following exception to this rule:

Balconies, decks or porches with a usable area of less than 20 square feet (1.86 m²) are not required to have a receptacle installed.

Clarifications:

- The 2008 requirement is a supplement to, not a replacement of, the requirements in effect in 2005. The 2008 NEC lists them both.

- The newer requirement does not necessarily require installation of additional receptacles in new construction. Depending on the location of the balcony, deck or porch, a single receptacle may comply with both requirements.

- Inspectors should not call out the lack of exterior receptacles as a defect in houses that were built before the code was enacted. Inspectors can recommend that receptacles be installed as a safety measure.

Reason for the 2008 Code Supplement

Extension cords are likely to be used to run appliances on large balconies, decks and porches (greater than 20 square feet) if receptacles are not installed at these locations. Extension cords can be dangerous, especially if used outdoors and in wet conditions. The dangers associated with extension cords are:

- structure fires. The Consumer Product Safety Commission (CPSC) estimates that extension cords cause 3,300 electrical fires every year in the United States. Common problems with extension cords that can lead to fires include:

1. overloading. This can occur when the wire gauge is not sufficient to carry the electrical load; and

2. short circuits. These occur where the current deviates from its intended path. For instance, if an extension cord becomes frayed, the hot and neutral wires may touch each other and the current would run down the wrong path.

- electrical burns and shocks. These are commonly caused by using old or damaged extension cords with broken or frayed insulation. The insulative sheathing in extension cords may tear away and expose the live wires. Ultraviolet (UV) light, to which extension cords are exposed when they are used outdoors, can hasten this process.

- tripping. Roughly half of the 4,000 injuries caused by extension cords annually in the U.S. are due to lacerations, sprains and contusions from tripping on the cords themselves.

Inspectors should note missing deck receptacles as a safety issue.

Weatherproof Receptacles

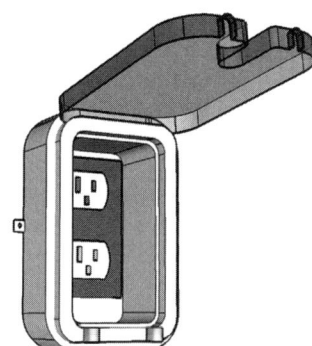

The image at left depicts a weatherproof receptacle cover. The deck receptacle should have a weatherproof cover.

As of 2008, the NEC requires at least one receptacle outlet on decks that are 20 square feet or larger.

Moisture Protection for Exterior Outlets

- The receptacle's faceplate must rest securely on the supporting surface to prevent moisture from entering the enclosure. If the receptacle is installed on uneven surfaces, such as stucco, stone or brick, a caulking compound can be used to fill in gaps.

- All 15- and 20-amp, 120/240-volt receptacles installed outdoors must have a weatherproof enclosure. These receptacles must also have a while-in-use cover.

- GFCI protection is required for all exterior receptacles, with the exception of this rare instance, as described by the NEC:

    GFCI protection isn't required for a fixed electric receptacle supplied by a dedicated branch circuit if the receptacle isn't readily accessible, and the equipment or receptacle has ground-fault protection of equipment.

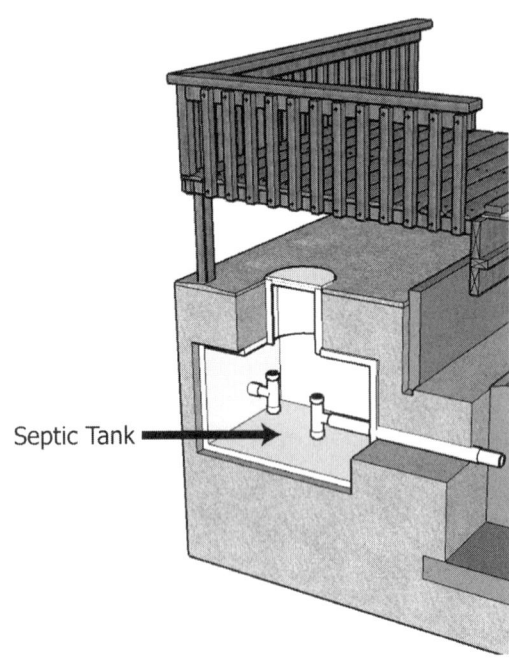

Septic Tank ──►

The image at left depicts a deck located above a septic tank access. Decks should not be located where they might obstruct septic tank accesses, underground fuel storage tanks, well heads, or buried power lines.

The image at right depicts a deck obstructing a basement bedroom's emergency egress window. Egress openings under decks and porches are acceptable, provided the escape path is at least 36 inches in height, and the path of egress is not obstructed by infill or lattice.

Quiz 5

1. T/F: Balusters can be used in place of posts if there is adequate infill between them.

    ☐ True

    ☐ False

2. T/F: The end-grain of vertical posts and balusters should be cut level.

    ☐ True

    ☐ False

3. Each segment of deck planking should bear on a minimum of _____ joists.

    ☐ two

    ☐ three

    ☐ four

4. T/F: Deck planking should be laid together as tightly as possible.

    ☐ True

    ☐ False

Answer Key is on page 38.

Appendix I: Answer Keys

Answer Key for Quiz 1

 1. A common safety issue found during a deck inspection is a lack of **guardrail infill**.

 2. A non-graspable handrail is a **safety concern**.

 3. T/F: A deck, unlike a balcony, can be constructed as a freestanding feature of a house.
  Answer: **True**

Answer Key for Quiz 2

 1. T/F: Most people congregate on decks near railings, so the deck load is often unevenly distributed.
  Answer: **True**

 2. The "7-Foot Rule" states that there should be at least 7 feet between **the bottom of the footing and daylight**.

 3. Posts in contact with soil should be **pressure-treated**.

 4. T/F: Posts should be connected to their footings so that the posts don't lift out or slip off.
  Answer: **True**

Answer Key for Quiz 3

 1. Painting deck posts can **hide** wood decay.

 2. T/F: Using the pick test, decayed wood will pull away with a lot of splinters.
  Answer: **False**

 3. T/F: Using the pick test, structurally sound wood will make almost no noise.
  Answer: **False**

Answer Key for Quiz 4

 1. T/F: Girders should bear directly on posts.
  Answer: **True**

 2. A "hammer test" checks for **loose fasteners**.

 3. T/F: Ledger boards can be adequately supported by stucco or brick veneer.
  Answer: **False**

Answer Key for Quiz 5

 1. T/F: Balusters can be used in place of posts if there is adequate infill between them.
  Answer: **False**

 2. T/F: The end-grain of vertical posts and balusters should be cut level.
  Answer: **False**

 3. Each segment of deck planking should bear on a minimum of **four** joists.

 4. T/F: Deck planking should be laid together as tightly as possible.
  Answer: **False**

EDUCATION & TRAINING BOOKS

Whether you're new to the business, an inspector seeking more information, or a veteran of the industry looking to expand your knowledge, these official InterNACHI publications will help you become the best inspector you can be.

We Offer the Following Education & Training Books:

- **How to Inspect the Exterior**
  Item Number: 0094

- **How to Perform Deck Inspections**
  Item Number: 0029

- **Residential Plumbing Overview**
  Item Number: 0064

- **Inspecting HVAC Systems**
  Item Number: 0061

- **Safe Practices for the Home Inspector**
  Item Number: 0038

- **Inspecting the Attic, Insulation, Ventilation & Interior**
  Item Number: 0109

- **How to Perform Electrical Inspections**
  Item Number: 0023

- **How to Inspect Pools & Spas**
  Item Number: 0076

- **How to Perform Roof Inspections**
  Item Number: 0042

- **How to Perform a Mold Inspection**
  Item Number: 0022

- **How to Perform Radon Inspections**
  Item Number: 0028

- **Inspecting Foundation Walls and Piers**
  Item Number: 0065

- **25 Standards Every Inspector Should Know**
  Item Number: 0037

- **How to Inspect for Moisture Intrusion**
  Item Number: 0073

- **International Standards of Practice for Inspecting Commercial Properties**
  Item Number: 0016

- **Structural Issues for Home Inspectors**
  Item Number: 0059

The purpose of these publications is to provide accurate and useful information for home inspectors in order to perform an inspection of the various systems at a residential property. They also serve as study aids for InterNACHI's online courses, as well as reference manuals for on the job.

Find these books plus more tools to grow your inspection business at
www.InspectorOutlet.com

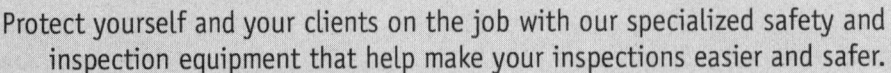